MILLION DOLLAR DAYS

Bigger Financial Possibilities and Big Table Moves

by Coach Micheal Burt

Million Dollar Days
*Bigger Financial Possibilities
and Big Table Moves*

Copyright © 2025
Micheal Burt Enterprises, LLC.
All rights reserved.

Other books by Coach Micheal J. Burt which can be
ordered at www.coachburt.com:

8 Figure Skills Stuck in a Six-Figure Vehicle
Everybody Needs a Coach in Life
Person of Interest
Million Dollar Follow Up
SWAG
Inside the Mind of a Monster
Living with a Monster

Cover Art & Interior: Navigation Advertising

Table of Contents

Introduction
Is It Possible For You?

When I was a high school teacher and coach one of the biggest statements I consistently heard from other teachers was, "We don't make enough money." Many teachers associated their low payment with being under valued but couldn't see a bigger future and many wouldn't even pursue a bigger future. This is how MANY people think, but this wasn't me. Something inside me told me different and that the skills I was accumulating by being a high school basketball coach combined with the confidence I was accumulating could be worth millions in the future. At that time I never believed or even imagined it could be worth a million per day or multiple millions per day but I saw a bigger future in my mind. I just didn't know what that future was yet.

Although I never made more than $55,000 or so in a single year and was working approximately

320 hours per month I always had a *commercial instinct and a high need for achievement* to do more and become more. As much as I valued helping young people deep down I believed I was a *Level 10 person stuck in a level four vehicle.* I had a big engine with a lot of horsepower looking for the right vehicle to put it in to. It took me 17 years of running a high performance coaching business in corporate America to locate that vehicle and surprisingly enough it wasn't in the coaching business, but utilizing the coaching business to meet the right people who introduced me to the right vehicles. This is why asking if your current vehicle can get you to your financial goals is always a good starting point, even before you actually get started. For the purposes of this book the vehicle represents the business you choose to go in to that allows you to distribute your abilities through for commercialization of those abilities and monetization of those abilities.

You see, very few of those teachers ever considered using their talents and skill sets they had accumulated over the course of their life time and turning them into profit generators. A good teacher many days is a therapist, a conflict resolution expert, a motivator, a problem solver, an innovator, a keeper of the peace, and a good coach all in one. All of these skills could be monetized both inside and outside of the education realm but very few could get past the title of "I'm just a teacher" mindset and "what else could I do?" Many times when I heard this statement about money I would ask a question that looked like this, "Do you know who Hal Urban is?" They would respond, "No, I've never heard of him." I would then say "Hal Urban wrote a book specifically for his children called "Life's 20 Greatest Lessons" that he self-published. That little book got out in to the public markets and he sold over 250,000 copies out of his garage. At a profit margin of $10 per book Hal made approximately $2.5 million dollars on his intellectual property or more. They would say, "Wow." I then would say, "Guess what Hal did for a living? He was a high school teacher." Looks like teachers can make millions of dollars if they activate their skill sets in new ways. You too can ACTIVATE a skill set you have in a bigger and more commercially viable way if you just open the mind to it... This book and philosophy will help.

Enter the $4 Million Dollar Teacher

Many years I speak on a cruise usually through the Eastern Caribbean. On the last one while in the airport I picked up several books that piqued my interest. One was "The Smartest Kids in the World and how they got that way" by Amanda Ripley. I've always been fascinated at how poorly we train young people to thrive in a modern and competitive world. In the book she takes a hard look through the eyes of three students who went in search of the best education in the world through foreign exchange programs. What they found was fascinating. In Korea there is a teacher named Andrew Kim. He earns $4 million dollars per year and is known as the "rock star teacher." He teaches in Korea in a private after school program called a Hagwon. He is paid based on one thing; demand for his skills and he was in high demand. Andrew Kim works about 60 hours per week but only teaches three in-person lectures. The internet turned his class rooms into commodities. Each lecture he did went online where students could purchase it for $3.50 per hour. Roughly 150,000 students watch his lectures online yearly. He has become a brand, not just a teacher.

This has got to become you if you want to experience Million Dollar Days. You are a brand, not just somebody out in the world with little or no skills. You are a specialist, not a generalist. You are being paid for your skills and the size of problem those skills solve.

This small handbook is a book about opening your mind to leveraging your skills and talents in much bigger ways. In the last month I've had multiple MILLION DOLLAR days with stock that I own in a company that went up $2 million in one day and raising capital for my Blue Marlin Capital fund that invests in data centers where we were raising over $1 million per day. It was in a healthy and positive way as well with little or no stress. All of this happened based on a formula I am now refining that I originally wrote about in my book *Eight Figure Skills stuck in Six Figure Vehicles*. Much of my coaching these days focuses on activating you, your business, and ultimately your wealth based on what I've learned and put in to action going from a high school teacher and basketball coach to an eight figure entrepreneur.

When I wrote the book (Eight figure skills stuck in Six Figure Vehicles) I had figured out how to generate more in ONE day than I used to in 365 days but hadn't yet figured out how to generate over one million dollars in a single day. *But I have now and I'm eager to share this new knowledge with you.*

You need to know that I'm not Microsoft, Apple, or Google. I have a small team of less than five full time employees. Now that I've figured out how to generate over one million dollars in a MUCH EASIER WAY I will put my mind to generating

$5 to $10 million in a day, and it is POSSIBLE.

This formula I've been using focuses on just three core components that I can teach you:

1. The locating of your *primary skill* that can be condensed down to ONE single word which gives you tremendous clarity over which problem you want to tend to and which ones you are most qualified to solve

2. Finding a *CORE problem* that is much bigger and more lucrative to use your skill to solve or an ambition you help another with where there is much bigger financial gain

3. Locating the right *VEHICLE* to place your skill into which represents how you distribute your skill to the world and are compensated for that skill in an EASY and RELAXED manner vs. ANXIETY FILLED and HARD. We are looking for FUN money vs. HEADACHE money.

But none of this will happen for you if you have this language internally:

1. I could never create one million dollars in a single day

2. I'm stuck in this vehicle I'm in and can't get out

3. I can't locate my primary skill

4. I can't stay focused on creating the right relationships

This is the Language of Losing.

I'm trying to re-orient you to have *The Language of Winning* that looks like this:

1. If he can do it I can do it

2. What's my version of what he is doing

3. I am highly skilled and have a big engine

4. I'm open to new opportunity vs. closed to it

5. Luck favors me because I'm alert, curious and responsive

Now, what's it going to be. Losing or winning?
Playing or spectating? Whining or acting?

It's your move... Now, let's learn the game.

Chapter 1
Eight Figure Skills Stuck in Six Figure Vehicles

At 25 years old I was a high school basketball coach. I was earning around $32,000 per year or something like that and loving every second of it. I was studying under Dr. Stephen Covey and mastering Covey's methods and using them to inner engineer my players and build "Competitive Intelligence" in my teams. I would soon find out that this KNOWLEDGE and these SKILLS and my HUNGER could be utilized in a different vehicle, specifically the skills of activating a drive inside of the players and instilling a belief in them that they could achieve more and become more. Turns out this skill transcends sports teams.

I was consistently getting the same question (which showed me I had something of value) that looked like this, "What are you doing with those kids?" What they were really asking was, "How do you get them to play so hard for you which such chemistry, discipline, and positive attitude?" I didn't have time to explain it so I wrote a simple book called "Changing Lives through Coaching." Now I had an asset, not in the book but in a message. People of Interest have a *MESSAGE*, a *BIG MISSION*, a lot of *MOVEMENT* and ultimately a *MONETIZATION machine.*

The message got me speaking engagements and the speaking engagements got me in front of people. It was here that I could SHOWCASE my skills of "inner engineering" and building "Competitive Intelligence" I was utilizing based on my deep mastery of Covey's work. Pretty soon people were asking me, "What would you charge me to work with my team?"

It started with $350 for three hours. It has moved to $35,000 for one hour but this still requires time for money (albeit it good money).

I would find out many years later that this skill of inner engineering (what we call today as "activating the PREY DRIVE") and using Competitive Intelligence could be used to coach CEO's and earn

stock options in companies to help them grow or up list and that stock could grow by over ONE MILLION dollars in a single day. Jackpot.
I also learned that I could exchange my skill to help companies drive enterprise value for a piece of equity in the company or a percentage of the exit.

Same skill used in a different application.

Let me say that again. *Same skill used in a different application.*

Baking Soda

Many years ago I coached some of the top whole life insurance specialists in the world. One of my favorites was named Phil Cavender. He was a master at presenting an idea and used props to explain different utilities in the usage of insurance. In this case he was showing people that insurance could be used to build cash value in a whole life insurance policy (sorry Dave Ramsey) and you could get the cash value and the death benefit simultaneously. During his presentation Phil would hold up a can of baking soda and ask,

"Do you know how we used to use baking soda?" He would then say, "To bake." He then would move the baking soda to his other hand right in front of the prospect and say, "How do we use baking soda today? To deodorize."

Same product just used in a different application.

I want you to think this way.

You can use your same skills in a different vehicle. You can use your same skills to solve a bigger problem. You can use the same skills to solve multiple problems. You may not have a skill problem but rather a vehicle problem or you simply don't know your skills. Or you have a confidence problem.

I like to say there are two types of problems with people"

1. Attitudinal: Don't want to do the work or don't believe you can do it.

2. Skill: The skill is not strong enough or mis-applied.

Ask yourself which problem you have?

What can we learn from chapter one:

1. I found a mentor who sharpened my skills and studied under him for eight years until I moved in to mastery. I didn't dabble with my skills. I found them and put them to work.

2. I used what I learned to differentiate myself from my peers. They were teaching basketball plays. I was teaching life skills and inner work.

3. I had a BIG ENGINE and a COMMERCIAL INSTINCT for more. I knew there was some BIGGER TABLE for me to sit at.

4. I used the Language of Winning vs. Losing.

5. I began to use my primary skills in a different application that could compensate me at bigger levels. This started me on a new path solving bigger problems that would pay me at a much higher level.

What's your primary skill and what is a BIGGER problem you can solve or a BIGGER ambition you can add your skills too right now?

Let's go to work. The Big Table is calling you.

Chapter Two:
Revelations—Converting Reputational Capital to Real Capital—My First MILLION Dollar Day

Many years ago I had a problem in my coaching business. I was generating thousand of leads but with a small sales force we simply couldn't get to all of them. This drove me crazy. Many have problems in their businesses but never do anything but complain about these problems. I began asking big questions like "Did I want to expand the sales force or did I want to find a strategic partner?"

I met with a coaching company in Nashville, TN that had 300 coaches who could sell and coach and only got compensated when they sold and coached. My thinking was I could bring the leads and they could bring the infrastructure. Together I believed we could make millions and potentially move toward an acquisition of my company with this strategic acquirer. I love the coaching aspect of helping people move from A to B but find myself not liking the business of coaching, including selling, follow up and conversion, and the problems that come along with human emotions. The coaching business is a nice to have, not a must have which makes it much harder to sell. It's hard to sell people on an intangible and can be grueling over the years to continue to show up and deliver for people only for them to have to "think about it." Some appreciate it and some don't and many leave you when you help them make money and believe they can do it without you. This is a vehicle problem you'll hear me talk about throughout this book. Some vehicles are much harder than others to build, grow, scale or exit. Look for must have businesses vs. nice to have. These are businesses that people have to have to survive vs. some emotional want.

My plan here was to ultimately say, "You pay me $1.7 million per year to do nothing but drive leads and coach and you handle everything else." We would share in the back end profits in some way and I believed we could do $25 million+ annually in a very short period of time. This would

represent a quantum leap for me and them.
This is how I want you thinking. Bigger plays, key partnerships, and accelerated paths vs. incremental and slow growth.

The deal didn't work out but the negotiating did and the first impression was a positive one. I met the president of the company named Dustin Hillis and we had a good exchange. I remembered him and he remembered me. He had since moved on from the company to become a key leader at a new company called Safespace, an AI technology company that was in the business of saving lives through patented AI technology that fills gaps in safety in healthcare, prison systems, transportation systems and more to keep people safe. This company has a big upside and a mission large enough many could fit in to, the sign of a great company from my perspective.
They also accumulated highly skilled team members, patented technology, and a big problem, keeping people alive through new technology that helped to build a safe space.

Through a mutual re-connection a few years later Dustin Hillis said, "Coach Burt I'd like to come see you with a big opportunity." He and Scott Boruff, the founder of Safespace showed up one day at my Greatness Factory and said, "Would you like to be an investor in the company, originally named HealthCare Integrated Technologies?" They asked me for $100,000 and said, "For one million you could be on the board of directors." I said, "Would you rather have my money or my influence?" Scott Boruff appropriately said, "Both" and we all laughed. I said, "Let me think on this but in the meantime I'm speaking here tomorrow at a capital raising bootcamp. Come see me speak and we can talk afterword."

The next day I was on fire. When you know you know. I pushed and challenged and captivated the audience that particular day with both Scott and Dustin sitting on the front row. It was a big hit for me and the audience and I was grateful for the opportunity. Scott and Dustin came to me on the break and said, "We have to meet with you right now." We stepped in to The Money Lab, a unique and curated room at The Greatness Factory where they said, "Forget the investment we want to ask you to be on the board of directors." And just like that I was given several million shares in the company for my skill of "activation," inner engineering teams, and helping people become "people of interest." Little did I know that my ability to "activate" people I had been using since my basketball coaching days could also be used to "activate" people to want a seat at a much bigger table and could be used to raise millions in new capital for companies looking to scale. Same skill, different application. Remember this formula.

In less than six months I had helped Safespace raise over $10 million dollars for runway and expansion with my skills and their hunger. I was asked to be on the board when the stock was at .6 cents. In less than six months through various strategies and their hard work and team application I woke up one day and it was at .90 cents. That 15X increase on that particular day resulted in my stock jumping almost $3 million dollars in ONE DAY. I went back invested more money as I believed in the company and the potential.

Now, that's how you have a million dollar day folks.

Since then we have put a plan together to get the company stock to $2.00 up-list to the New York Stock Exchange and ultimately $10.00 and then what will that stock be worth?

Let's de-construct this for your application. I call this converting REPUTATIONAL CAPITAL (the reputation you have built over a long cycle of time) + having a HARD SKILL to REAL CAPITAL (exchanging your reputation to raise capital to be put to use).

Here is how it shook out:

I had a problem and had a ceiling in my coaching business. I didn't stay there, I went looking for a strategic partner to solve this problem. Think QUANTUM LEAPS here that come from meeting a NEW PERSON or someone bringing you NEW INFORMATION.

I made a good impression in our first meeting and had a solid track record of demonstrated capacity and a business with over a million of EBITDA (it takes 21 positive interactions to overcome a negative first impression).

That first impression opened the door to a second opportunity that could become way bigger than opportunity #1. This is why you need to understand that all of the opportunities you are going to get will come through other people you meet and some will be unlikely partners that walk in to your path.

Investing in a company and being on the board of directors is much easier than running a coaching business, that is a very hard vehicle to scale.

I used the speaking engagement to showcase my skills "one to many" and they saw that the influence of speaking and activating could be worth way more than $1 million.

I exchanged my KASH (knowledge,, attitude, skills, and habits) for their CASH (stock options in the company). This is a Dan Sullivan concept called ***Total Cash Confidence.***

I then applied my PRIMARY SKILL to SOLVE a NEW PROBLEM of raising capital, strategic positioning, and helping to drive enthusiasm for the company (that other people are running).

My STOCK in the company went up almost $3 million in ONE DAY. On any given day this stock may be up 10-15x what I got in at.

Remember our formula:

1. Find your primary skill

2. Find the RIGHT PROBLEM you can solve

3. Place your skill to solve the problem in the RIGHT VEHICLE

The company is Safespace and can be found on the TICKER at SSGC (Safespace Global Corporation).

Chapter 3:
Blue Marlin Capital and the
INTRODUCTION to Quantum Leaps

Two of my top coaching students Nic Fields and Dr. Johnny Shanks spent over a year studying the rise of renting racks of data in a de-centralized structure. They came to me and said here's the problem, "There is more demand for storing data than there is supply and with the increase of AI and people wanting to pull their data from the likes of Microsoft and Amazon due to egress fees there is a big opportunity in raising capital, purchasing the racks of data and renting it." They formed a management company called DEDNA and got in the business of renting racks of data in managed data centers.

This is where the great Dr. Price Pritchett enters the equation. Price, whom I coached with throughout the 2025 year wrote *you2* and *The Quantum Leap Strategy,* two books about being open to and experiencing Quantum Leaps.

He's sold over $80 million in books and through his publishing division which in itself speaks to the power of his writings. He opened my mind to the world of "trying different vs. trying harder."
For the grinders out there you will want to pay specific attention here. You, like I believe in working hard to achieve a target. Price's books open the door to trying differently which opens a new part of the brain.

When studying Dr. Pritchett's work on Quantum Leaps (significant jumps in a business) he noted that many times a quantum leap DOES NOT COME in the field you are currently in (which is what many people try to do) but in another field somewhere out there. It may have NOTHING to do with the current field you are in. In the late 80's Price was doing executive assessments and became bored and disgusted with his incremental growth of his business. One day he walked in unannounced to his entire team they were going to get in to mergers and acquisitions as he considered this to be THE BIG TABLE, where the big boys and girls play. He said, "This was the biggest game in business." To that point they had never participated in a merger or acquisition. He saw an opening, a crack and he went for it. In less than six years he was considered the #1 mergers and acquisitions expert in the U.S.

Note these things when thinking about your business:

They had no training in mergers and acquisitions.

They had no brand in mergers and acquisitions.

They had never done a merger or acqusition.

He was a clinical psychologist who had ventured over to the business world, first in assessments and now moving to mergers and acquisitions. This was a CHOICE he made to move toward a bigger future. His staff was confused but he was CLEAR in his AIMING POINT. He was going to use his PRIMARY SKILLS to solve a MUCH bigger problem that he would be compensated at a much higher level for. Are you seeing this trend.

Same skill used in a different vehicle with much bigger commercial viability.

Within six years he was the #1 mergers and acqusition expert in the United States earning millions by picking a lane NOBODY was in and dominating it. While on the path he realized that just like a COMPANY could experience a QUANTUM LEAP so too could a person. This would prompt him to write you2 and The Quantum Leap Strategy, grossing over $14 million in book sales (which is unheard of in the publishing world).

As I pondered getting involved in the data centers I kept coming back to Dr. Pritchett. Be open to the possibilities that land in your lap. I followed up his first two books with one called "Lucky You," which breaks down how you drive up the probability of luck by moving and circulating, choosing a clear aiming point, and being open when opportunities fall right in to your lap, especially Level 10 opportunities.

So, one day Nic Fields called me and said, "Coach, what do you want to call our fund where we raise capital for these data centers?" I said, "That's an easy one. Let's call it Blue Marlin Capital." You can fish for BLUE GILLS in the local lake or you can fish for BLUE MARLINS in the Gulf of Mexico. I was ready to fish for BLUE MARLINS.

We set out to raise over $10 million dollars within 90 days and deploy 48% returns to the first fund investors meaning off every $100,000 invested in the data centers we sent them back $4,166.00 for an expected seven years. Now we were in business as the early investors started telling others and word spread like a wildfire that they could get predictable returns in concentrated periods of time.

This was the first time I had created my own fund.

This was the first time I had gotten involved with data centers.

This was a first for everything.

By day 90 of our first fund we were raising right at $1 million PER DAY. These were MILLION DOLLAR DAYS folks. I see us starting to raise $20 million on days coming up as in fund #2 we can promote on social and will be working with family offices (Blue Marlins) as well as individual investors.

Fund #2 is about to start and I'm excited to see it take off.

Let's de-construct how you can experience something like this:

1. Be open to the possibilities that you can use your current skills in a new vehicle.

2. Be open to the possibilities that sometimes NEW and BETTER opportunities fall right in your lap (See Pritchett's book "LUCKY YOU")

3. Be open to strategic partnerships where you partner with people have a specialized skill set and you marry your specialized skills with theirs. FIND YOUR WHO's.

4. Be open to new trends as your current business may be going against certain micro and macro economic trends and cannot get the traction that another business might can.

5. Ignore conventional wisdom that you should just "work harder" in your current vehicle and ride the wave of something that can RUN and RUN FAST.

Who are the BLUE MARLINS you need to be connecting to and who are the partners you need to be finding where you marry your skill set with theirs to create something magical?

Chapter 4
The Quantum Leaps and Quantum Thunderbolts

What I'm about to tell you to start this chapter is true. I can't make this shit up.

Sitting on a Southwest Airlines flight after a long day and bemoaning the flight attendants giving the same boring message (I'm sure they believe is common sense) again a passenger beside me opened up a bag and begin to eat barbecue chicken wings dripped in barbecue sauce. Surely in school somewhere along the way someone would or should learn that this is not the place to eat food like this. The gentleman had chicken wing sauce all over his hands, face, and then the seat. It was on this flight that I made a bold decision; ***I was going to buy a private jet.***

I 100% believe in life "where there is no pain there is no change." After hundreds of flights per year I was at my limit. I then needed to de-construct how I could get this plane and it actually wasn't as hard as people lead you to believe it is. Most that discourage you to do something in life have ACTUALLY NEVER done it themselves. Their limited think projects on to you causing you to doubt what you are capable of doing.

This is where most people stop. They have had enough of something in their lives but then allow the "cost" of something new to stop them so they justify where they are and just bitch about it.
Let pain fuel your Quantum Leap.

Get SICK of incremental growth.

Get SICK of having to watch what you spend and where you spend it.

Get SICK of under performance from people.

Get SICK of working hard to just get back to the same place.

When asked why Price Pritchett went in to mergers and acquisitions he said, "I was DISGUSTED with where we were playing."

The Quantum Leap is initiated through pain. After re-verse engineering how you have one of these Quantum Leaps I believe it happens through intentional **QUANTUM THUNDERBOLTS.**

A thunderbolt is a sudden and unexpected jolt of energy that you initiate. When you feel STUCK, PLATEAUED, and COMPLACENT what you or your team needs is a sudden and unexpected jolt of energy. This is a BOLD MOVE in a NEW DIRECTION.

I believe MILLION DOLLAR DAYS happen when you are utilizing the RIGHT SKILL to solve the RIGHT PROBLEM and you are in the RIGHT VEHICLE.

I also believe that Quantum Leaps happen when you:

1. Are interested to gain NEW KNOWLEDGE from someone that opens the mind to new possibilities. You have to pursue these people.

2. Meet NEW PEOPLE who open the door to NEW PEOPLE or NEW OPPORTUNITY and follow up on that opportunity.

So how do we initiate a QUANTUM THUNDERBOLT:

1. Raise your standards, don't lower them. Anyone not on the train that is moving fast or bought in to the vision has got to GO. The faster you get rid of them the better. If they are slow in thinking, action, or not fully committed and flexible in their thoughts they need to find another bus to be on. Don't wait on this. When you have to think about it make the move.

2. Don't stay in a VEHICLE that you know can't get you to the BIG GOAL for one minute. Either TORCH IT, TWEAK IT, or UTILIZE it as a feeder system to a better vehicle. You have non-refundable seconds (Bobby Castro) and every second in the wrong vehicle with the wrong vehicle cannot be recovered. Get unreasonable with your actions, your people, and your vision.

3. Think of WHO can help you MOVE toward your BIG targets faster. This could come from a key strategic partnership, a stage you need to be on, or an IDEA you need to initiate that is BOLD and RISKY.

4. When you have ideas or what Gladwell called "Blinks" go with them vs. suppress them. These ideas where the sub-conscious mind is telling you to move toward something can work. But it has 100% chance of not working if you don't work it.

A QUANTUM THUNDERBOLT for me

In 2014 I had a radio show called "Change your Life Radio." It was on a small radio station that nobody listened to in Nashville on the FoxNews affiliate. It was an A.M. station. My slot was Sunday's at 1:00 p.m. or so. I paid $15,000 for the spot for the year but what I ended up with was an opportunity to create a million dollar day. Think $15,000 investment + investment of my time and in less than four years created over $2 million dollars of new actual money. That's 133X improvement.

I was always looking for people to interview who had a point of view. While walking through the Chicago airport to a speaking engagement I saw a book that lined the walls called *10X* by Grant Cardone. I had no idea who Cardone was but I liked the concept and he seemed like a guy I would like. Bold. Gritty. Moving.

I called his office and asked to interview him. He had a new book out and was always looking for promotion and took the interview. We hit it off and this would start somewhat of a professional friendship.

In 2018 it was time for 10X 2 at Mandalay Bay. I was in Grant's office and asked him a pointed question, "Do you think I'm good enough to speak at 10X 2?" He answered with, "Yes you are but you're not famous enough. I paid $4 million to rent Mandalay Bay and I need to put some butts in the seats." I then said, "Okay what if I helped you put some butts in the seats by buying $100,000 worth of tickets?" He thought that would help him and help me get me on that stage. It was a BOLD MOVE, or what I call a PREY DRIVE MOMENT. In this case it was a QUANTUM THUNDERBOLT.

I didn't have a talent problem. I had a marketing problem. I had an obscurity problem. I needed the world to see me and that stage opened that door. I crushed it that day on stage in front of that audience. We would generate roughly $250,000 in the first hour or so and I would go on to generate over $2 million from that stage and that hour. This started with a $15,000 investment that returned over 133X the investment. through ONE KEY RELATIONSHIP. The key to the MANY is the ONE...

That Million Dollar Day started with some simple decisions:

1. I need to get in front of people. I am highly talented yet under capitalized.

2. I need to get better and I chose to have a radio show for promotion.

3. Getting on the radio show would introduce me to key strategic partners.

4. Activating the 10X stage would help me go on to meet Tim Grover, Tim Storey, and Ed Mylett and I would go on to partner with some of them in certain ways so we all got increase.

5. By betting on me and paying the $100,000 to activate the tickets I would gain an important confidence to know I could play on bigger stages in the future.

And oh yeah, I would package the $2,000 tickets, add my coaching program for one year + a private VIP party at the top of Mandalay Bay and sell them for $5,000.

I made $150,000 prior to even getting on that stage.

Listen to your gut. Make a bold move. Have a Prey Drive moment. Bet on YOU.

Now, I want you to identify 3-5 QUANTUM THUNDERBOLTS you can INITIATE.

These will not come to you. You will be the person who initiates the action here.

It's a bold move. It's a strategic play. It's a bold ask. It's a swing for the fence.

Chapter 5
The Big Table

While interviewing Dr. Price Pritchett,
Lewis Howes asked him a simple question,
"What prompted you to go in to mergers and
acquisitions?" Dr. Pritchett said two things that
would get my attention and create a true
trigger moment:

1. *I was disgusted with where we were which
   was good. We weren't making any mistakes.
   We were on auto-pilot.*

2. *I wanted a seat at The Big Table, and
   mergers and acquisitions is the biggest
   game in business.*

This answer prompted me to begin asking
questions. How could we define *The Big Table* and
I began giving it these definitions:

1. It's the biggest opportunities you are sitting
   on right now that you are not focused on.

2. There is a return on your time (You can get somewhere much faster)

3. There is a return on your energy (It excites you vs. depletes you)

4. There is a return on your investment (Money in or time in becomes big outputs out)

5. It is highly enjoyable (Business can actually be fun)

6. It is highly profitable (Big payouts can happen in this vehicle)

7. It is highly meaningful (This taps in to your purpose)

It you drew five boxes right now out on a piece of paper and you called them your "LEVEL 10 opportunities" what would they be? Do they fit in the box of the criteria I mentioned. What is the Big Table for you...

If I were doing this exercise as an example I would do it like this:

1. The coaching business I have has introduced me to MUCH of the BIG opportunities I have had in life but it is not The Big Table. There is too much commoditization and very hard to scale. It could be a deep feeder system to find strong and committed people for other things that could lead to bigger and bigger opportunities.

2. The private equity firm we have Pitch Equity could be a billion dollar fund if we really focused on it. Diluted focus could result in diluted results.

3. Blue Marlin Capital is going to raise millions for data centers and there are additional ways to monetize this that I believe are coming.

4. Safespace could get to $10 on the New York Stock Exchange and that stock be worth $30-$50 million in the future.

5. Scaling The Greatness Factory as deal factories or capital factories is a passion and can be lucrative both through the real estate and the deal flow. These "centers of influence" positioned by concepts pull in some of the top people in the world. These people want deal flow, new opportunity, and strategic partnership.

These are VEHICLES. The ones that get the most attention and time will expand as what gets attention grows. Water what you want to grow.

For you right now sit down and ask yourself some questions:

1. What results are you completely disgusted with?

2. What is the Big Table for you?

3. Who do you need to meet, get in a room with, learn from, or partner with to move toward this Big Table?

4. Can your current VEHICLE get you to where you want to go? Get brutally honest on this.

5. Is it time to TORCH, TWEAK, or UTILIZE your current VEHICLE and what's your first move?

It's time for you to step in to your potential and quit avoiding it. It's time for you to make the hard decisions to find The Big Table.

If I were making success simple I'd say it like this:

"Get to the right place, get around the right people, use your primary skills to solve the right problem." This leads to a Bigger Table and a million dollar day.

Chapter 6
Skill

The people who earn the most money are the most skilled. It's typically that simple. Nine out of 10 people can't articulate what their primary skill is and what problem they are uniquely qualified to solve. Many are solving BLUE GILL problems and getting paid BLUE GILL money. This places the skills in to what I call "general skills" that solve "general problems." The big money people are **specialists, not generalists.** They utilize their unique past to develop a hard primary skill to solve a much bigger problem for others. Always remember, *money changes hands when problems are solved*. The bigger the problem the more money people will pay to solve that problem. You have to become a must have vs. a nice to have. Nice to haves always get cut during tough economic times. Must haves very seldom get cut.

Think of your skills this way:

You help people achieve their ambitions.

You make the noise go away.

You are a needle mover.

You bring your unique skills to their equation for Quantum Leaps.

You bring an unmatched energy to the room that converts to money.

You see things other people don't see.

You find under capitalized assets and activate them.

You bring brands to life or activate brands.

You know how to get in the room with those who have money and resources.

You solve GIGANTIC problems..

Now, these are hard skills.

When you think about your skills I want you to think about your hard skills, not soft skills. Like personality is a soft skill. Having a good attitude is a soft skill. Being upbeat and fun are soft skills. Can you convert these skills to million dollar days, possibly? But what I've seen is that these skill may get you in the door but they don't keep you in the door. People who stay at the party are the ones who drive some kind of serious result.

A hard skill is a skill that is very hard to find. It's unique. It solves a very specific problem for someone. Think Maverick in Top Gun who comes in to fly a very specific mission that only HE can do. He may be only ONE of millions who can pull this off. He spent a life time cultivating that skill. What skill have you spent a lifetime cultivating that would be incredibly valuable for others?

Whatever income level you are currently at could indicate one of three things:

1. Your skill is not that strong or defined..

2. You are not solving a big enough problem..

3. You are clearly in the wrong vehicle.

4. You have a marketing problem or packaging problem.

5. You are swimming in the wrong pools with the wrong people.

Let's go back to my example:

At 25 years old I had the skill of activating potential in people and inner engineer people to WIN. I earned $27,000 per year or somewhere similar to utilize this skill to build young basketball players and win championships. I was really building identity, standards, language and accountability in to a culture that had never won at the highest levels. When I wrote my first book I went and spoke for a major company and they paid me more in ONE hour than I made in ONE month. I was speaking on how I inner engineered my players and built a culture around positive expectancy of winning.

I went home that night and asked these questions that I want you to ask yourself and KEEP asking yourself:

1. What skill do I have?

2. What problem did I solve?

3. Why would they pay me that much money?

4. Where can I do this again?

At 31 I would retire from high school sports making a record high $55,000 as one of the highest paid public school teachers in Tennessee. My first contract in corporate America was $75,000-$150,000 with bonuses so I was operating at a 3X clip. When I added a few more of those and got to $1,000,000 in revenue in essence I had 10X my income but I still wasn't hitting million dollar days.

I kept repeating the cycle:

1. What's my skill: Activation

2. Whats the problem I solve: Activating others to perform at a higher clip

3. What's the vehicle: A performance speaking and coaching business

I would go from $1,000,000 to $5,000,000+ but kept showing incremental growth until I started looking for how to use my skill to solve a different problem and find a new vehicle. Remember our baking soda analogy? We use our same skill in a new vehicle.

I then shifted my focus to:

1. Using my skill of activating people to get a seat at a much bigger table through activating them, activating their business, and activating their wealth.

2. I used my love of real estate with my love of coaching to build a new Greatness Factory

($8 million dollar complex). This attracted some of the best people in the world who had bigger vehicles that could scale much faster.

3. These "new strategic partners" invited me to partner with them.

4. I would then use my skill of ACTIVATION to activate a BRAND, ACTIVATE a CONCEPT, and ACTIVATE raising CAPITAL.

The new and bigger plays all revolved around the same skill: Activation.

This is the same skill I was using to activate potential in young people, activate potential in business people, and now activate a brand or concept.

Same skill utilized to solve a bigger problem. Think Baking Soda.

Where did the skill come from?

A combination of who I studied under (mentors and coaches), life experiences of activating people and teams, and real life experiences of conceptualizing a concept and bringing it to life. *All of this came from my past...*

Remember, I'm paying you for your PAST.
Your PAST helps me to BUILD my FUTURE...

Now, it's your turn.

What is your PRIMARY HARD SKILL? This is a real skill that solves a real problem or helps create something.

What is a MUCH BIGGER PROBLEM you could solve and for whom?

What VEHICLE should you be distributing your talents through to solve the problem?

Do the deep work here to go deeper on this concept and write it up over and over until you have clarity on this and do a deep discovery on your skills.

People who experience Million Dollar Days always have incredible strong skills. Think MAVERICK... He was probably only one of five people who could have pulled that mission off on Planet Earth.

This is a very important thing to understand so pay close attention. People are paying you for your one thing; your SKILL. It does not matter what you sell. All of those are commodities. Separate yourself with your skill level and let us help you package that skill in a better way so you can command top dollar for that skill.

Chapter 7
Fall in LOVE with Problem

I don't remember when I started saying,
"Money changes hands when problem are solved"
but somewhere along the way I did and it's true.
Many times the only reason a person parts with
their hard earned money is because they have
either something they want (an aspiration) or some
kind of problem they want to get rid of. And the
problem drives the spending

Employers hire employees to solve problems..

People use your product or service to help them
solve a problem...

If the problem is small then there is very little
monetary gain unless you solve the problem for
millions of people.

Many years ago one of my clients said to me that
there are only two types of businesses:

High volume with low profit or low volume with high profit.

For example I could work with ONE client who paid me a million dollars or I could work with 10 clients who paid $100,000 or I could work with 1,000 clients who paid $1,000 dollars.

You have to decide what primary skill you have, what problem you are uniquely qualified to solve, and what vehicle you want to distribute it through.

Many fall in love with an idea. They try and sell that idea of what they have fallen in love with. The founder of Waze app which helps you navigate traffic said that he fell in love with the problem.

You see he lived in another country and only had two ways to get in to work. Many days he didn't know where all of the traffic would be on his route so he would call ahead to his friends and they would "report back" which road was better. This was a problem. He decided to build an app that reported the problems, the traffic, and the best way to move from point A to B. He sold that company for $1 billion dollars.

The size of the problem determines the size of the paycheck. We call these big players "Blue Marlins," which represent big fish. As a reminder we call the big opportunities Level 10 opportunities.

I've solved a lot of problems in my life time. Some paid $99 per month and some paid me millions of dollars in shorter periods of time. The last time I looked my house in Florida had appreciated by roughly $2.3 million. They say you make money when you buy, not when you sell. I bought off market at 2.3% interest rates and held the house through various economic cycles. My ultimate goal is to sell at the right time, pocket a few million and then move on up to the beach. Where I live in Florida (Watercolor) the beachfront houses start around $10 million and off the beach range from $3-$9 million.

The only reason a person buys or sells a house is that they have an ambition (to make money) or a problem (they don't like the house they have or need to get rid of it).

So, let's begin asking ourselves what problem could we totally fall in love with? I like to say, "Just because we can solve a problem that doesn't mean that is the problem we are supposed to be solving." I hear this a lot from really smart people:

"You are powerfully positioned to help the person you used to be."

I somewhat agree with this statement but what if the person you used to be doesn't have any money?

I used to be a high school basketball coach. I thought it would be natural for me to just "go back" and help those people but here was the problem, they didn't have a lot of money to give me for my help.

I quickly figured out that I could take my skill of activation to corporate America and they could pay me 10X what those basketball coaches could pay me. I figured out that raising capital, activating entire brands, driving up the enterprise value of a a company for exit, and creating intimate experiences for people could pay me the kind of money I was looking for. None of these people I was helping in these scenarios are people I "used to be."

What if we changed the phrase of, "You are powerfully positioned to help the person you used to be" to this, "You are most powerfully positioned to help the person who you were but really wanted to become actually become what you wanted to be."

I remember being young and hungry and had a big engine.

I needed to understand monetization, raising capital, scale, exits and roll ups, and expansion. I was willing to pay good money to learn these things because I had a burning desire to become something new.

Now, let's get back to BIG PROBLEMS. Your payout will be in proportion to the size of problem you solve and the amount of money you help another person make.

If you came to me and said I'd like to scale your Greatness Factories around the world and spin them up but all you wanted was a % of the profits I'd be open to it. You see in some of my deals I get a percentage of equity for my skill set and the real returns don't kick in until the exit. It's a gamble I'm willing to take if I'm playing with the right people. I'm not married to the idea, I'm married to the person and if that person has shown a demonstrated capacity to win I know they will figure out how to win.

I marry their skill set with my skill set and we AMPLIFY the results.

Here's how we know if you have real skills and can solve a real problem. Could we drop you off in any city in the United States with only $100 to your name and you can't use any of your previous connections and you build or add $1 million in new revenue to a company in less than 90 days. Say what you want to about Grant Cardone but he proved he could do this in the reality TV show *Undercover Billionaire*. He formed a strategic partnerships in one of the worst economic cities in the U.S. in Pueblo, Colorado in a national recession due to Covid and built a business valued at $5.5 million in less than 90 days.

If you have a real skill and you are a specialist at solving the right problem you should be able to join ANY COMPANY and be a NEEDLE MOVER in a quick period of time.

You come in. You diagnose the problem. You solve the problem. Imagine if you could have Million Dollar Days by adding $25 million to the top or bottom line to a company within 90 days. Now, that's a skill I would be interested in acquiring in you.

Companies in my opinion have one of three problems:

1. A leads problem (could be marketing)

2. A conversion problem

3. An engagement and delivery problem

Everything else is NOISE. I've seen people with supposed good skills come in to companies and actually create revenue problems when this is the #1 thing a person should solve for a company. You may solve that problem by solving the marketing problem or the leads problem but this is an important problem to solve. If you accept a job as the Chief Revenue Officer of a company you need to move the revenue needle. That is your WHOLE JOB.

When the university of Alabama hired Coach Nick Saban to be their new football coach many people in Alabama complained that he was the highest paid employee of the state of Alabama at $32 million for eight years (what small thinkers).

In year #1 they brought in $95 million through the football program as a result of hiring one person, Saban.

Not a bad bet to pay someone for eight years and 3X your money in year one.

What problem did he solve? Apathy. Average. Disengagement. Losing.

He brought "positive expectancy" and results to the equation. He has now leveraged those skills in to car dealerships, TV deals, licensing deals and much more.

Here's what I want you thinking from this chapter:

1. What is the perfect fit for your skills and the perfect problem you want to solve?

2. If you could solve a BIGGER problem with your primary skill what would it be?

3. Who would stroke you the biggest check for your skill set today and in the future?

4. What problem could you truly fall in love with?

5. Are you excited about the current problem you are solving and the people you are solving it for?

Here's what I see the most:

1. Many don't know their skill.

2. Many don't know their problem.

3. They are in the wrong vehicle.

If this is YOU then it's time to TWEAK it, TORCH it, or UTILIZE it to find the perfect combination of these three things.

Chapter 8
Locating the RIGHT Vehicle

If I had to go back many years to being a young man and I had to be coached and trained on one thing it most likely would be "choosing the right vehicle." Just this week we brought in a bright young man who went to Michigan and then Vanderbilt who chose to get in to the Private Equity game, specifically of acquisition and roll ups (putting companies together to roll them up and sell as one unit). While he was speaking I was thinking, "Man I should have gotten in to that vehicle because that's where the big money is."

The truth is I wouldn't change anything about my path as I went in to my calling. The vehicles I chose early in life didn't have any thought about scale or exit and that's okay as they led me to what I do today. But I do wish I would have gotten some coaching on:

1. How to build a business that could be sold for a liquidation event (Real wealth begins with a liquidity event)

2. How to get over in to the investing side early

3. How to raise capital

4. How to negotiate at a very high level

5. How to get close to power sources and multipliers

6. How to build, grow, and scale an idea

7. How to create businesses that are "needs" vs. "wants"

8. How to hire and attract the best talent that is the right fit for your organization that can move the needle

9. How to hyper scale

10. How to use technology as an accelerator

11. How to become an incredible marketer and market at scale to produce thousands of leads

I went the other way. 80 hour work weeks. Hand to hand combat. Small and boutique thoughts. And then I started studying Quantum Leaps that should be easier, free flowing, trying differently vs. trying harder. I wrote "Eight Figure Skills Stuck in Six Figure Vehicles" which outlines the formula we've been drilling in your brain in this book (by the way the average person will only retain 80% of what they learn if they hear it 6-8X in a 48 hour period). This is why repetition is necessary in coaching.

That formula is:

1. Skill

2. Problem

3. Vehicle

The vehicle is so important to this equation. Think and ask yourself these questions.

Is the vehicle I've chosen:

1. Scalable

2. A need vs. a want

3. Sellable

4. Has Recurring revenue

5. Is Recession proof

6. Is Easy

7. Is Hard

8. Is Dependent on me or a team

Remember the Level 10 Opportunity is:

1. Highly Enjoyable (Fun and possibly easier)

2. Highly Profitable (Big margins or lots of scale)

3. Highly Meaningful (Fills both internal profit and external profit)

The coaching vehicle, in the way I chose to do it, was:

1. Not scalable

2. A want vs. a need (making it very hard to sell)

3. Not sellable with few economic buyers and would still need me

4. Had some recurring revenue but mostly project based income

5. Not recession proof but really hard to sell when in a recession (I've been through three)

6. Not easy, but very hard

7. Too dependent on a few key people (like me)

Now, having said this I've LOVED most of the coaching business and it's helped me to build my wealth and given me and my family a better life than we EVER IMAGINED. But then it did something else, it opened my eyes to where the much bigger plays could be and became a FEEDER system to a network of like minded achievers who wanted to:

1. Invest in our private equity fund PITCH EQUITY which purchases under capitalized assets in business and real estate

2. Invest in our Blue Marlin Capital funds which invest specifically at the time of this writing in Data Centers through the Blue Marlin Data Fund

3. Invest in Safe Space which is the publicly traded company I'm on the board of directors of which uses multi modal AI technology to keep people and institutions safe

4. Host events at our various real estate assets like The Greatness Factory or The Lodge

In essence the VEHICLE has produced positive cash flow that I used to:

1. Invest in real estate around the country

2. Build a Greatness Factory

3. Create funds people can invest their new profits in to

4. Build key strategic partnerships that lead to bigger deals

So the PRIMARY VEHICLE was better than my FIRST VEHICLE of being a high school basketball coach but I NEEDED the first vehicle to build my SKILL.

This lead me to find a BIGGER PROBLEM of taking my PRIMARY SKILL in to corporate America and creating positive cash flow through a new business (speaking and coaching). This new VEHICLE, although hard and sometimes difficult led me to meet the right people to form key strategic partnerships to be able to create MILLION DOLLAR DAYS... Everything was feeding everything, not always intentionally but in retrospect.

Now, there are coaching companies that have millions dollar days like Tony Robbins or Grant Cardone but both of those people have used the vehicle of coaching to create bigger vehicles like REAL ESTATE or being involved in 30-200 more companies (Like Robbins).

So, with your current vehicle you can do three things:

1. USE IT and MAXIMIZE it to create bigger profits and re-invest those in to the current company.

2. TORCH IT and tear it down because it just ain't working and does not fit in the box.

3. TWEAK IT which means to "strategically pivot" the business and change the focus or strategy of the company to more specialization or to re-position the business to become a feeder system to bigger opportunities.

So, here's a question for you:

Can your current vehicle experience Million Dollar Days in its current form?

Or how would you like to utilize this vehicle for a bigger play? Possibly this vehicle could become a feeder system to your bigger opportunities? Open the mind to these bigger possibilities.

Now, it's your turn. Let's tackle these questions:

1. Does your current vehicle meet your goals both internally and externally?

2. Can the current vehicle get you from A to B?

3. Is the current vehicle the RIGHT OPPORTUNITY or a FEEDER SYSTEM to the right opportunity?

4. If you were to TWEAK the current vehicle how would you tweak it?

5. Do you need to TORCH parts of the current vehicle or the entire vehicle?

6. Can your current vehicle experience Million Dollar Days?

7. Where is the LIQUIDITY event for the current business?

8. What would need to happen structurally in the current vehicle to set it up to experience a QUANTUM LEAP?

Chapter 9
Relationships—The Key to the Many is Through the ONE

When I look back at virtually EVERY Quantum Leap I've ever experienced it happened as a result of just a few things:

1. A genuine curiosity about improvement and expansion

2. Key movements and circulation with a primary skill toward the action

3. The meeting of ONE new person who had INFLUENCE or KNOWLEDGE who wanted to acquire or utilize my skill to assist them toward a bigger goal

4. That ONE person introducing me to a NEW GROUP of people

5. Those people BUYING my products or services or INTRODUCING me to NEW people who came in to my network or investing in our various funds

When you hear me say, "You don't need more money you need more people" this is the reason.

If you go back to our formula for this book and much of my coaching it all starts with a SKILL.

The skill builds demand and you have a desire to commercialize this skill for monetization by using it to help and assist others. You began to package, market, and promote your skill to the world. This introduces you to NEW people. You begin to meet new people and these people introduce you to their people. You also meet people who have NEW KNOWLEDGE and some of them become GAME CHANGERS for you.

They bring you new knowledge and energy.

They open new doors for you.

They allow you in to their networks.
Their networks become part of your networks.

Therefore, "The key to the many is to the ONE."

One relationship could change your life.

One relationship can open a new door.

One relationship can help you have a bigger financial future.

But, that one relationship won't happen unless you move and circulate and have a skill and solve a real problem.

Today should be about FINDING YOUR GAME CHANGERS and moving toward them. It should be about building and forming strategic partnerships that move the needle. It should be about using your skills to negotiate a seat at a much Bigger Table. I strongly recommend Jana Creel's new book who is on my team "Proximity to Power" which shows you what to do and not to do when approaching people of power and influence. More people screw this up vs. get it right and this costs them millions in new opportunities.

This is also where Prey Drive comes in. The ability to see something with the eyes or in the mind and move toward it with a persistence and intensity. To wake up daily and pursue your goals while knowing that those goals are going to be achieved in and through others, not alone.

So how do we find our ONE? I use a system we teach our students called "Tactical Connection," which is a series of movements and organization that places me at the table..

I have a message: Everybody deserves a seat at a much bigger table.

I have a mission: Helping people secure that seat at a much bigger table.

I have a lot of movement: Through the Tactical Connection System.

I have a monetization model: Let me coach and mentor you, partner with you, invest with me, or host an event at one of our locations (Greatness Factory or Lodge).

The Tactical Connection system and the way I map out my weeks starts with my Prey Drive Planner which you can download here: https://planner. coachburt.com/

It places key relationships in to buckets that look like this:

1. The Level 10 opportunities- The biggest opportunities available to us that we need to be focused on.

2. The Blue Marlins- The biggest relationships we should be focused on.

3. The Hit List- New money opportunities which could come from current clients, past clients, key strategic partnerships, and direct leads (that must be called).

4. The Farm Club- People who are interested but have not been closed and need to be nurtured.

5. The Red Zone- People close to making a buying decision and need information and courage.

6. The Top 25- Deep and KEY relationships you need to nurture and invite to something in the future.

7. The Showcase- Key activation points that drive people to something where there is a buying decision. These are events you can invite people to.

I typically work to have 35-57 touches per day in this system. I touch, tag, invite, encourage, and convert when I'm doing my touches. This takes Prey Drive and skill. Most struggle with both. The conversion of an opportunity to monetization is a specialized skill that many need to develop.

Every Million Dollar Day opportunity I've talked about in this book "fell in to my lap" by practicing this system I've outlined in this book and FINDING my ONE…

Here's my challenge to you to close this chapter:

1. Be open to possibilities that are right in front of you. Don't ignore them or be closed off to them.

2. You most likely have your ONE's in your network that you are not paying attention to. The brain doesn't focus on the big opportunities available to it unless you tell it to.

3. Skill up and go in to battle daily and good things will happen. Money and opportunity follows movement.

4. Now, let's go in to your plan.

- Where do you need to be circulating?

- Who do you need to be following up with?

- Who are your Blue Marlins?

- What are your Level 10 opportunities?

- What skill are you bringing to the party and who would want it?

When you study ANY Million Dollar Day performer they all say the same things: It all comes down to relationships....

Find your ONE that can introduce you to the MANY and QUIT spending time with those who can't help you move from A to B.

Conclusion

You need to know that Million Dollar Days are available to you if you continue working the muscle and tweaking the vehicle and practicing what is in this book. Become obsessed with the vehicle you are in and the relationships you are building. Be open to new opportunities and know that your Quantum Leap may not be in the current vehicle you are in, it may be in using your skills in a new and exciting way.

Now, get out of mental creation and in to physical action.

I'm fighting for you...

See how I can help you at coachburt.com and get to the right place and around the right people, which I think is at THE GREATNESS FACTORY...
See more there at www.thegreatnessfactory.com